MIX
Papier aus verantwortungsvollen Quellen
Paper from responsible sources
FSC® C105338

Uwe Bußmann
Silvia Schweighofer
Robert Marc Panz

Organisational Cultures

Networks, Clusters, All ances

Anchor Compact

Bußmann, Uwe, Schweighofer, Silvia, Panz, Marc Robert: Organisational Cultures:
Networks, Clusters, Alliances. Hamburg, Anchor Academic Publishing 2013
Original title of the thesis: Organisational Cultures

Buch-ISBN: 978-3-95489-121-4
PDF-eBook-ISBN: 978-3-95489-621-9
Druck/Herstellung: Anchor Academic Publishing, Hamburg, 2013
Additionally: Essen, FOM – Hochschule für Oekonomie und Management, Deutschland

Bibliografische Information der Deutschen Nationalbibliothek:
Die Deutsche Nationalbibliothek verzeichnet diese Publikation in der Deutschen
Nationalbibliografie; detaillierte bibliografische Daten sind im Internet über
http://dnb.d-nb.de abrufbar

Bibliographical Information of the German National Library:
The German National Library lists this publication in the German National Bibliography.
Detailed bibliographic data can be found at: http://dnb.d-nb.de

All rights reserved. This publication may not be reproduced, stored in a retrieval system
or transmitted, in any form or by any means, electronic, mechanical, photocopying,
recording or otherwise, without the prior permission of the publishers.

Das Werk einschließlich aller seiner Teile ist urheberrechtlich geschützt. Jede Verwertung
außerhalb der Grenzen des Urheberrechtsgesetzes ist ohne Zustimmung des Verlages
unzulässig und strafbar. Dies gilt insbesondere für Vervielfältigungen, Übersetzungen,
Mikroverfilmungen und die Einspeicherung und Bearbeitung in elektronischen Systemen.

Die Wiedergabe von Gebrauchsnamen, Handelsnamen, Warenbezeichnungen usw. in
diesem Werk berechtigt auch ohne besondere Kennzeichnung nicht zu der Annahme,
dass solche Namen im Sinne der Warenzeichen- und Markenschutz-Gesetzgebung als frei
zu betrachten wären und daher von jedermann benutzt werden dürften.

Die Informationen in diesem Werk wurden mit Sorgfalt erarbeitet. Dennoch können
Fehler nicht vollständig ausgeschlossen werden und die Diplomica Verlag GmbH, die
Autoren oder Übersetzer übernehmen keine juristische Verantwortung oder irgendeine
Haftung für evtl. verbliebene fehlerhafte Angaben und deren Folgen.

Alle Rechte vorbehalten

© Anchor Academic Publishing, ein Imprint der Diplomica® Verlag GmbH
http://www.diplom.de, Hamburg 2013
Printed in Germany

Executive Summary

"The organisation network consists of different nodes and interconnections of the participating network partners. In relationship of their mutual interactions these interconnections, which transmit power, information, money or raw material, are loose or tight", defines Thorelli in 1986 (Thorelli 1986, p. 37 ff).

By means of the mutual interactions of the organisation network one or several markets are covered. Thus, the network has to be strategically organised according to the common organisation network strategy and additional factors.

In general, the field of activities of the network members overlaps to a certain degree. In this respect especially three areas are important:

- the type and field of business
- the range of products or services
- the attracted field of customers

The less the overlapping of activities the higher is the chance for synergetic effects inside the organisation network and the better is the stability of the network connections.

External and internal reasons are important for the development of organisation networks:

Major external reasons are the progress of information technology as well as the distribution of the Internet, which lead to the development of social networks. Often these social networks are the basis for the development of organisation networks.

On the economical field, which is driven by the external reasons and impacts a fast change of market's and customer's demand. This fast change claims to flexible productions on international markets at last, which are additional external reasons for the development of organisation networks.

Major internal reasons for the development of organisation networks are the need for companies to meet the changing demand by a fast corporate introduction of innovations and optimised costs and quality. Unless this important goal could not be achieved by own corporate strength the company has to optimise its structure by building an intra-organisation network, join an inter-organisation network or build alliances with other companies.

After covering the local market, the single company has to go international. There are several strategies for an international approach. According to Sain an international organisation has to develop its own corporate strategy in the following way (Sain 2009, p. 23):

- Develop the core strategy. Base for sustainable strategic advantage.
- Internationalising the core strategy. Through international expansion of activities and adaptation of the core strategy.
- Globalising the international strategy. Global integration.

More improved forms of international business offer the transnational company, which becomes an Integrated Network in its optimised form.

By joining inter-organisation networks the single company becomes part of a regional network / cluster or a strategical network according to Sydow (Sydow 1992b, p. 252). The major importance of a strategical network lies in its strategical leadership by a large-scale enterprise. Consequently, the business area the network is engaged in is predominantly determined by this enterprise.

The Japanese Keiretsus are well-known examples for strategical networks.

The literal interpretation of the term cluster says in general that it is a mass of single components which are forming a whole. Schramm-Klein (2005, p. 535 f) noted that there is no standardised determination for the term cluster because of the great variety of interpretations. In economics literature that deals with the topic strategic management you will almost exclusively find the interpretation of Michael, E. Porter for the term cluster. This assignment will be also based on the definition of Porter.

Porter (1998, p. 4) defined cluster as "geographically proximate groups of interconnected companies and associated institutions in a particular field, linked by commonalities and complementarities".

Business clusters are more than an accumulation of alike companies. Having a first view at a business cluster, you may associate the following with the members of the cluster (Schiele 2003, p. 27):

Members of a business cluster are companies that …

… are more profitable than others in their business
… all belong to the same business
… are all located in the same region

On the one hand this first view approves the definition which is basis of this part of the assignment, the definition of Michael E. Porter. On the other hand there is one new fact that has to be analysed, the association that members of clusters are more profitable or let us say more successful than others.

Demanding customers, rivalling companies, competitive suppliers and supporting infrastructure makes cluster members more competitive than others. Companies outside the cluster often realise the demand for innovation too late because they do not feel the force to develop their products and services at such an early stage as the cluster members do.

In times of globalisation the question arises: Is it possible to form an international business cluster? Over and over again you read and hear about local clusters. Being local, in a geographical proximity is also an important fact for the definition of the term cluster.

Schiele (2003, p. 72) did not find any really existing international clusters. He pointed out that geographical proximity has also a cultural dimension. Therefore international clusters are not formed.

Globalisation demands the internationalisation of cluster. That means that clusters should support their members in doing international business. Therefore, the cluster is often part of an international network.

Strategic alliances can take a variety of forms, ranging from an arm's-length contact to a joint venture. But the core of a strategic alliance is an inter-firm co-operative relationship that enhances the effectiveness of the competitive strategies of the participating firms by the trading of mutually beneficial resources such as technologies, skills, etc.

Typical Alliances are:

- Sales Alliances
- Solution-Specific Alliances
- Geographic-Specific Alliances
- Investment Alliances
- Joint Venture Alliances

The 'Pyramid of Alliances' gives an even detailed view on this subject.

To make an alliance work, the whole alliance must be integrated in the company's strategy of all participating firms.

But how to prepare an alliance? Business expert Larraine Segil suggests an easy to follow 15-step-plan to prepare a strategic business alliance.

In some industries, alliances have been the standard for a long time.

Carmakers mainly use alliances to:

- manufacture certain car parts
- combine their R & D activities
- concentrate their sales activities

Another industry were alliances are common is the airline industry. The airlines focussed mainly on strengthening and expanding their market presence through providing transport possibilities to ample destinations around the world.

At the moment there are three major airline alliances existing worldwide:

- Star Alliance (24 partner) (Star Alliance 2009)
- Sky Team (13 partner) (Sky Team 2009)
- oneworld Alliance (10 partner) (oneworld 2009)

In the future there will be some difficult global problems to tackle. These challenges can only be solved by cross border acting strategic company alliances or/and strategic alliances with or between governments.

But not only the 'big problems' are a challenge for firms, the competition in nearly all business sectors is getting tougher every year. To be even more competitive as the competitors, further cost reduction and new business solutions are in demand.

Therefore, the number of alliances will definitely grow further in the subsequent years.

Table of contents

Executive Summary V
Table of contents IX
List of Abbreviations XI
List of Figures XI
List of Tables XII
1   **Problem Definition** 1
2   **Objectives** 1
3   **Methodology** 1
4   **Networks** 2
   4.1.   What is an Organisation Network? 2
   4.2.   Reasons for Organisation Networks 4
      4.2.1.   External Reasons 4
      4.2.2.   Internal Reasons 6
   4.3.   Types of Organisation Networks 8
      4.3.1.   Intra-Organisation Networks 8
      4.3.2.   Inter-Organisation Networks 14
5   **Clusters** 18
   5.1.   What is a Cluster? 18
      5.1.1.   Cluster – The Term 18
      5.1.2.   Dissociation from the Term Network 19
   5.2.   Strategic Business Clusters 20
      5.2.1.   Formation and Types of Business Clusters 20
      5.2.2.   More than an Accumulation of Alike Companies 21
      5.2.3.   Cluster Membership as Strategic Advantage 23
      5.2.4.   International Business Clusters? 24
   5.3.   Examples for Business Clusters 24
      5.3.1.   Cluster EnergieForschung.NRW 25
      5.3.2.   ACstyria Autocluster GmbH 25
6   **Alliances** 26
   6.1.   What is an Alliance? 26
   6.2.   Difference between Alliances 27
      6.2.1.   Primary Differentiation 27
      6.2.2.   Pyramid of Alliances 27
   6.3.   Integration of Alliances in Companies Strategies 29
   6.4.   Preparation of a Business Alliance 30

		6.5.	Examples for Strategic Alliances	33
		6.5.1.	Automobile Industry	33
		6.5.2.	Airlines	34
	6.6.		Future of Alliances	35
7	**Results**			**36**
8	**Conclusion**			**37**
9	**Bibliography**			**38**

List of Abbreviations

AG – Aktiengesellschaft (i. e. public company)
BOAC – British Overseas Aircraft Corporation
cf. – compare
CO_2 – carbon dioxide
e. g. – for example
etc. – and so forth
f – the following page
ff – the following pages
ibid. – to be found at the same place
i. e. – that is
LTU – LTU International Airways
MAN – MAN AG (i. e. Truck Manufacturer)
NIKI – NIKI Luftfahrt GmbH
NRW – North-Rhine Westphalia
OEM – Original Equipment Manufacturer
p. – page
R&D – Research and Development
VW – Volkswagen AG

List of Figures

Figure 1: Networks – here social networks (Source: Verst 2009) 2
Figure 2: The Integrated Network (Source: Bartlett, Ghoshal 1990, p. 119) 12
Figure 3: The Mitsui Keiretsu (Source: WTEC 2009) 16
Figure 4: Network strategies (Source: Sydow 1992a, p. 27) 17
Figure 5: Development of local business conglomerates (Source: Own interpretation) 19
Figure 6: The Determinants of National Advantage (Source: Porter 1998, p. 72) 22
Figure 7: Members of ACstyria (Source: ACstyria.com) 25
Figure 8: Pyramid of Alliances (Source: The Lared Group) 28
Figure 9: Airline Alliances in 1999 and 2009 (Source: Own Interpretation) 35

List of Tables

Table 1: Organisational characteristics (Source: Bartlett, Ghoshal 1990, p. 92) 10

Table 2: Regional and strategical networks (Source: Sydow 1992b, p. 252) 14

1 Problem Definition

There are big problems coming towards single companies nowadays. The progress of information technology and the distribution of the Internet as well as the changing demand of customers, especially for no standardised products force them to react immediately.

Their problems are:
- How can they reach the state of flexibility to meet the changing demand?
- How can they compete within a market with increasing innovations of products and decreasing product life-cycles?
- How can they acquire the necessary capital, technology and know-how to compete?
- How is it possible to optimise their corporate structures and achieve synergetic effects?

2 Objectives

The objectives of this assignment are to help the single companies out of their miserable situations and to present them interesting answers to the questions raised above. Of course these answers are already in use and approved by reality.

3 Methodology

- Reference book research
- Internet research

4 Networks

4.1. What is an Organisation Network?

Today networks become more and more omnipresent in daily life: In private life people join social networks to communicate, establish friendships, find partners etc., in business life they work with computer networks, the corporate intranet and the Internet. Thus, especially the information technology has coined the term "network" and defined it as a "logical alignment and type of interconnections between communication partners in a net, which transmits communications inside or outside a building." (Sellien 1988, p. 570).

Figure 1: Networks – here social networks (Source: Verst 2009)

This definition serves as a basis for business administration, where several approaches to the term organisation network exist.

Organisation Networks

Thorelli made a very good and well accepted approach in 1986. He defines, "the organisation network consists of different nodes and interconnections of the participating network partners. In relationship of their mutual interactions these interconnections, which transmit power, information, money or raw material, are loose or tight." (Thorelli 1986, p. 37 ff).

By the means of the mutual interactions of the organisation network one or more markets are covered. Thus the network has to be strategically organised according to

- the common organisation network strategy.
- the positioning of the single companies inside the organisation network.
- the positioning of the different brands.
- the diversification.
- the market channels.
- the vertical integration, which means integration of up- and downstream manufacturing levels.
- internationalisation.

In general the field of activities of the network members overlaps to a certain degree. In this regard especially three areas are important:

- the type and field of business
- the range of products or services
- the attracted field of customers

The less the overlapping of activities the higher the chance for synergetic effects inside the organisation network is and the better the stability of the network connections are. So in fact there is a small competition between the network members, but no real resource competency. Consequently the network members keep their autonomy of decision.

4.2. Reasons for Organisation Networks

4.2.1. External Reasons

In the post-industrial society a lot of fundamental changes of the corporate environment happen, which lead to the development of the complex but flexible corporate structures of organisation networks. Alter and Hage identify five general effects, which are especially responsible for the increasing constitutions of networks (Alter, Hage 1993, p. 38 ff):

General Effects:

1. The progress of information technology and the distribution of the Internet and their diffusion into daily life have a major effect on the development of organisational networks.
   By these means people become informed about nearly any information or news all over the world. This knowledge offer people new opportunities of creating new social fields and positioning inside. They want to exchange and discuss the new information of their fields of interest with new communication partners, who are interested in these fields, too. The meeting of partners with a common field of interest by the new means of communication constitutes social networks, which are the basis for organisation networks.

   In these social networks people exchange information about personal or professional content. Consequently any field of interest is enlarged and intensified by any new participant.

   Examples of social networks are the Internet communities of
   - Facebook.de, Stayfriends.de for the personal type or
   - Xing.de for the professional type.

2. Nevertheless the rapid technological development, which leads to the growth of knowledge and know-how causes a high increase of technological complexity, too, which is the second major effect for the increasing number of organisation networks. Thus the technological complexity in the production processes as well as the economic risk for the single company has to be distributed on additional partners.

3. The third effect for the development of organisation networks is the changing customers demand, especially for non-standardised products. This implies the necessity to

change the corporate alignment from the efficiency output of large standardised quantities to more flexible and specialised productions.

Consequently the maintenance of large-scale effects on the one hand in combination with a flexible production which quickly reacts on the market demand on the other hand, is a very high challenge. This challenge could only be met by organisation networks.

4. The understanding of the needs and the advantages to work together promotes the mutual trust of companies, which establish the basis for qualified organisational relationships. This is the fourth effect for the development of organisation networks.

   In general the relationship between companies is determined by competition and distrust. But due to the development of this new culture of trust, the number of cooperations and organisation networks is increasing. Especially in Japan this organisational culture of trust has been cultivated for years, which is the reason for Japanese cooperation competency in form of the well-known Keiretsus.

5. The fourth factor leads to the fifth one, which has its origin in Japan, too. Especially in this country the government took influence in the economic activities of the companies. This took place in the seventies, when the Japanese government directly controlled the product line of the companies. Consequently economical goals are subordinate to political goals, which prevented a free market economy.

Economic Effects:

These external effects lead to changes on the economical field. In detail Alter, Hage (Alter, Hage 1993, p. 13 ff), Wildemann (Wildemann 1998, p. 47 ff) and Sydow (Sydow 1995, p. 13 ff) pointed out the following economic changes, which in turn cause an increase of organisation networks:

- the growing internationalisation of the market- and trade relations
- the increasing dynamic of innovation of products
- the fast change of the market's- and the customer's demand
    - the fast change of technique, values of society etc.
- the market entry of new industrial nations, like China and India
- the shortage of resources
- the growing demand towards producers and suppliers
- the need to concentrate on core competences

All of these aspects require a fast adjustment of the company and advance the development of organisation networks. They offer flexible structures and the possibility to combine different business activities to cope with the changing circumstances.

4.2.2. Internal Reasons

The security and the expansion of the competitive position of the company are dependent on the corporate ability to react flexibly on the changing market situation. That means the changing demand is met by a fast corporate introduction of innovations and optimised costs and quality.

But these strategical competitive advantages could not be achieved by an increasing of the own corporate productivity at least. Thus it is necessary to combine the own corporate strategical strengths with the strategical strengths of other companies to reduce the complexity of the value chain.

After all the reasons for companies to establish organisation networks is the big opportunity for them to complete their corporate weaknesses with the strengths of other companies and offer in return their corporate strengths to complete the others' weaknesses. According to Thorelli companies try to gain the following strategical strengths (Thorelli 1986, p 40):

Strategical Strengths:

- financial strength
- technological strength
- expertise / know-how
- legitimacy / trust

In this regard the meaning and importance of the three first strengths are obvious. Trust between companies is often constituted by social networks, personal relationships or friendships. It is the base for long-term contracts inside organisation networks.

Powell evaluates these strategical strengths and transforms them into the following concrete economical goals of single companies (Powell 1987, p. 71):

By joining an organisation network the single company pursues the goal

- to get faster access to new technologies and markets.
- to benefit from the economies of scale by common production or research and development.
- to access company-external know-how.
- to diversify the risk.
- to use common synergetic effects.

4.3. Types of Organisation Networks

These goals could be achieved to different degrees by the different types of organisation networks. In this connection the types could be established according to intra- respectively inter-organisational aspects of the corporate structure and to the strategical or regional corporate orientation.

4.3.1. Intra-Organisation Networks

According to the changing conditions of competition a change in the corporate structure has to be initiated. In order to reduce the complexity of the production reorganizational measures have to be taken first inside the company.

The traditional hierarchical structure has to be renewed by modularisation and decentralisation of corporate divisions. This corporate restructuring provides small but flexible units, with decision-making authorities and profit responsibilities for their own.

The Module Organisation

Osterloh and Frost (Osterloh, Frost 1996, p. 96 ff) define the modular organisation as a segmentation of the company into particular units, which are in technical and economical respect autonomous.

These single modules build one structured, decentralised network, which consists of
- production modules, like
    - the cost centre,
    - the service centre,
    - the profit centre and

- administration modules, like
    - the management centre and
    - the competence centre.

A precondition for this module organisation is the coordination of the modules, which
- results from their own self-organisation.
- is granted by special measures, like orders, arrangements or transfer prices.

The flexible modules equally interact with each other as an intra-organisational network. By these means the module organisation is well adapted to the new competitive conditions. Nevertheless after covering the local market in the first step, it has to enlarge its strategy internationally and expand to an international organisation.

The International Organisation

The growing internationalisation of the markets pushes companies to compete abroad and to achieve cost advantages internationally. For this purpose the company needs a key for a successful global strategy.

According to Sain a company, which expands internationally has to develop its corporate strategy in the following way (Sain 2009, p. 23):

- Develop the core strategy. Base for sustainable strategic advantage.
- Internationalising the core strategy. Through international expansion of activities and adaptation of the core strategy.
- Globalising the international strategy. Global integration.

By these means the adapted core competences of the parent company is internationally applied. The know-how of the parent company is transferred to the international branches abroad. This is an advanced approach for the company to international success.

The Transnational Company

In contrast to the International Company the branches abroad of the transnational company are interdependent and specialised, which offers additional local advantages. Thus, integrated worldwide activities are possible for optimized coverage of the local markets.

By these means the company enlarges its corporate core strategy to develop multinational flexibility, global compliance and international competitiveness.
This most optimized approach to international markets provides the company the big opportunities

- to establish strong local branches under consideration of the regional demands and markets.
- to achieve cost advantages by the integrated world-wide activities of these branches.
- to acquire and apply world-wide know-how by these branches.

Bartlett and Ghoshal named a company, which combines all of these characteristics

Transnational Organisation

(Bartlett, Ghoshal 1990, p. 32 ff).

The following table gives an overview about the different corporate approaches to the international market.

Organisational characteristics	Multinational	Global	International	Transnational
Configuration of resources and skills	Decentralised and independent in the national context	Centralised and world-market oriented	Centralised core competences, other competences decentralised	Widespread, interdependent and specialised
Function of the branches abroad	Identification and utilisation of local market opportunities	Realisation of strategies of the parent company	Adaptation and Application of competencies of the parent company	Differentiated shares of the international branches for integrated worldwide activities
Generation and diffusion of know-how	Acquirement and saving of know-how in any unit	Acquirement and saving of know-how of the parent company	Acquirement of know-how in the parent company and transfer in the overseas branches	Common acquirement and application of know-how

Table 1: Organisational characteristics (Source: Bartlett, Ghoshal 1990, p. 92)

Thus the three key elements determine the transnational organisation:
- the allocation of organisational responsibilities develops flexibility
- the local marketability enables understanding of the customer demand and flexible reactions
- organised learning processes improve innovations

The transnational organisation is determined to react on complexity and change. It is adaptive, flexible and becomes highly competitive by its good learning ability. The corporate resources and skills are specialised but widespread and independent, which means any branch abroad gets its particular function and responsibility inside the organisation network.

The Integrated Network
Consequently this complex variety of different branches, functions and responsibilities have to be clearly distinguished and well-coordinated to achieve optimum output.

The integration of all of these functions into an organisation network is characterised by Bartlett and Goshal the

Integrated Network.

(Bartlett, Ghoshal 1990, p. 119).

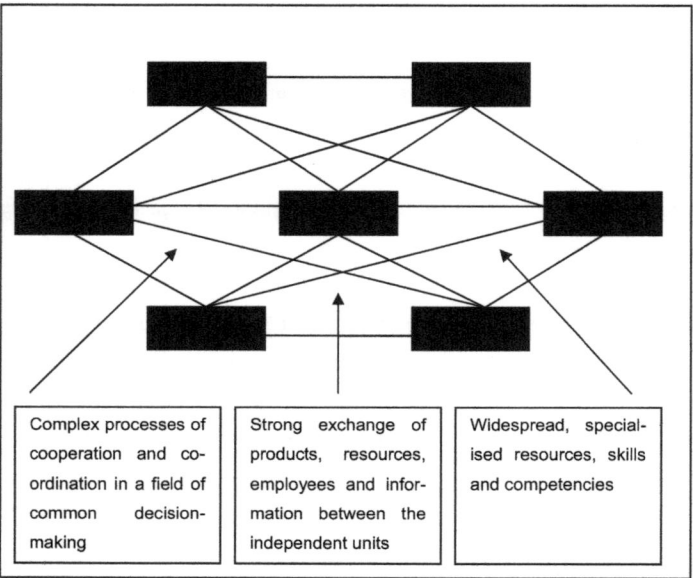

Figure 2: The Integrated Network (Source: Bartlett, Ghoshal 1990, p. 119)

The advantage of the integrated network is

- world-wide corporate resources, skills and competences could be strategically allocated and favourable and low priced employees, resources and technologies could be easily integrated into the network. Thus the branches get their strategical function inside the network by the meaning of their skills, resources, know-how and their local markets.
- the shortening of the product life-cycles as well as the rapid change of costs, technologies and customer preferences is met by the flexible corporate productions adapted to the local markets.
- the corporate sales and distribution are aligned to the local culture and market.
- the corporate economical risks could be minimised by distribution inside the product portfolio.

Beside the opportunity to expand from one local market to several markets by building a corporate intra-organisation network the single company has two other opportunities:

- The second opportunity in the field of networks is to participate in an Inter-organisation Network.
- The third opportunity, which stands outside the field of networks and is therefore slightly different from the second one, is to build alliances with other companies abroad. This big opportunity is explained in the last chapter in detail.

For all three opportunities the international alignment is still increasing.

4.3.2. Inter-Organisation Networks

There are two major, well accepted types of inter-organisation networks differentiated by Sydow (Sydow 1992b, p. 252):

- Regional networks
- Strategical networks

The following table points out the differences:

Inter-organisation Networks	Regional Networks	Strategical Networks
Company size	Small- and medium-sized companies	Companies of different sizes
Strategical leadership	Without the strategic leadership of a single company	Strategical leadership by a large scale enterprise
Company structure	More emergent, informal structure	More intentional, formal structure
Network relationships	Changing network relationships	Stable network relationships
Geographical distribution	Regional concentration	Regional and often international distribution

Table 2: Regional and strategical networks (Source: Sydow 1992b, p. 252)

Regional Networks

In the economics literature the term "regional networks" is simultaneously used with the term "business clusters", which the following chapter is dedicated to.

Strategical Networks

The major importance of strategical network of companies of different sizes lies in their strategical leadership by a large scale enterprise. In this context strategical leadership means the long-term development and protection of those economical potentials of the organisation network, which are of major competitive importance to strengthen the market position.

Consequently the business area the network is engaged in is predominantly determined by its leading large scale enterprise:

In this way it constitutes the strategical directives, the inter-organisational relationships, the assignment to value adding and supporting companies and finally the common approach to the market (Sydow 1992a, p. 23 ff).

Examples of Strategical Networks

Japanese Keiretsus

They are characterised by an inner circle of Keiretsu companies, which is lead by a large-scale enterprise as central company and an outer circle of subcontractors:

The inner circle of Keiretsu companies
- access different markets.
- has interdependent minority interests to strengthen the inter-organisation relationships.
- provides common capital investment planning
- is debt financed by the banks of the Keiretsu
- performs an interchange of capital between the network companies
- performs a transfer of technology
- performs a transfer of the board of managers

The outer circle of subcontractors are
- small family companies, which execute personnel-intensive tasks.

The strategical network companies are competing, although often cooperations in basic research are made. All members are tight by loose contracts, which drive their readiness for cooperation. Because of their mutual dependences on unique supply relationships, detailed contract are not necessary.

Whereas the inner circle of the Keiretsu is dependent on the expertise of production and innovation of the outer circle of subcontractors, this one is economical dependent from the inner circle.

Consequently the strategy of the strategical network is the flexible specialisation, which is the basis for the development of many strategical networks in the USA and in Europe, too.

Examples of Keiretsus

Mitsui-, Mitsubishi-, Sumitomo-, Fuyo-, Sanwa-, DKB-Group

The following figure reveals the interdependences of the Mitsui Keiretsu.

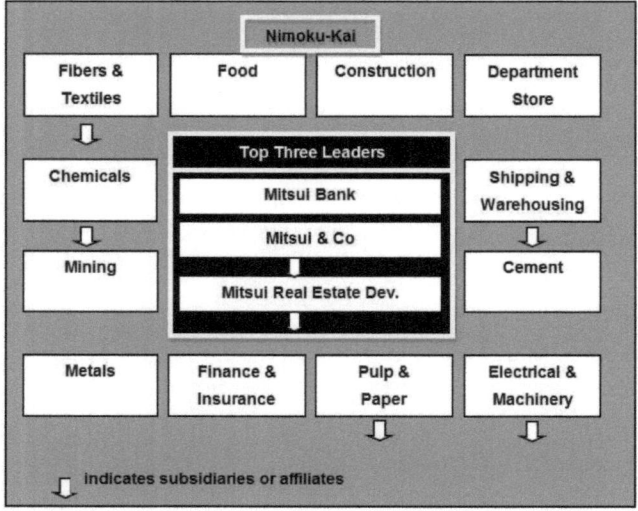

Figure 3: The Mitsui Keiretsu (Source: WTEC 2009)

Strategies of Inter-Organisational Networks

Sydow identifies two strategies of inter-organisational networks (Sydow 1992a, p. 27):

- the strategy of differentiation
- the strategy of cost-leadership

The Strategy of Differentiation

An organisation network that pursues the strategy of differentiation builds cooperations with companies to combine research and development, share the modern technological production and the distribution channels, which are aligned to the common consumer targetgroup.
In the automobile branch the strategy of diversification is promoted by the relationships between producer and subcontractors.

The Strategy of Cost Leadership

By following the strategy of cost leadership any function which is not core competence or any personnel-intensive function is outsourced. By this way the relationships to the subcontractors become more and more important. To manage this network an efficient controlling system has to be implemented.

The following figure gives an overview about both strategies:

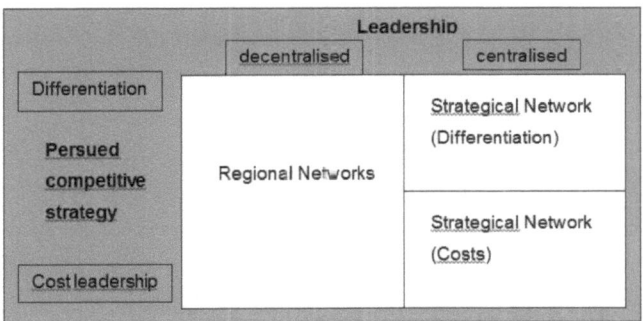

Figure 4: Network strategies (Source: Sydow 1992a, p. 27)

In fact both strategies, the strategy of diversification, as well as the strategy of cost leadership could be applied simultaneously.
Mercedes Benz e.g. leads a strategical network with Chrysler in the USA on the one hand, and on the other hand it systematically cooperates with regional networks in Baden-Württemberg.

Because of this simultaneous application a differentiation between strategical networks and regional networks according to the different strategies is not possible.

However the following chapter about "clusters", which are used in literature simultaneously to regional networks gives a deep insight and reveals the differentiation...

5 Clusters

5.1. What is a Cluster?

There are different meanings of the term cluster. The actual literature shows various explanations which will be discussed in the following. This provides the basis for the decision which definition will be used for this assignment. The dissociation to the term network is very important to find a clear definition for clusters.

5.1.1. Cluster – The Term

The literal interpretation of the term cluster says in general that it is a mass of single components which are forming a whole. In music they talk about clusters if they mean a sound formation that consists of chordal intervals (Langenscheidt 2009). In mathematics a cluster analysis is used for showing a accumulation of variables in complex data records (Duden 2006, p. 182).

To meet the focus of the module in which this assignment is written it is important to find an economic, scientific interpretation of the term cluster. Already in 1905 Marshall (p. 290) talks about a local concentration of small and mediums sized companies in a specific industry that are connected to each other through the value-added chain (1905, p. 290). Perry (2005, p. 78 f) wrote about Marshall's Industrial Districts that the members of the districts were more competitive than companies outside the district. Similarities were also found in the company's strategy and the innovation of the industrial district members.

GREMI a group of social scientist named the idea of creating innovations in networks Innovative Milieus. They hypothesised that innovation cannot be realised alone in companies or their surroundings. The members of an Innovative Milieu are managers, scientists, lecturers and politicians. They all are interacting in their social and business networks. The strength of the Innovative Milieus is the interference of the private and the business networks of their members (Perry 2005, p. 25).

Schramm-Klein (2005, p. 535 f) noted that there is no standardised determination for the term cluster because of the great variety of interpretations. In economics literature that deals with the topic strategic management you will almost exclusively find the interpretation of Michael, E. Porter for the term cluster. This assignment will be also based on the definition of Porter.

Porter (1998, p. 4) defined cluster as "geographically proximate groups of interconnected companies and associated institutions in a particular field, linked by commonalities and complementarities".

The following figure will visualise the development of above described local business conglomerates:

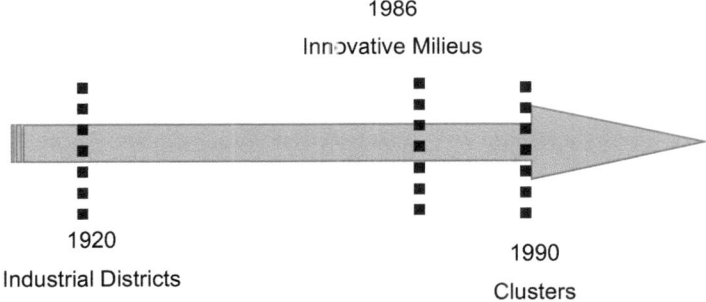

Figure 5: Development of local business conglomerates (Source: Own interpretation)

Having this definition of Porter in mind, chapter 5.3. goes into detail how a business cluster works today.

5.1.2. Dissociation from the Term Network

Strategic networks and cooperation are more and more topics of business-people discussions. The term network is clearly defined in chapter 4.1.of this assignment. Here we will focus the dissociation to the term cluster.

In the actual topic related literature the terms network and cluster are often used as synonyms. But for this assignment it is important to show the, perhaps small but essential, difference between these two terms.

Networks, even strategic ones and cooperation can be parts of a cluster. There are two functions which you can only find in a cluster. A cooperation or a network does not offer these functions.

The first function of a cluster is the organisational form of it. It is in its collectivity an organisation between market and common structure. A cluster is an organisational form that comprises networks, cooperation, alliances and other market orientated organisations. This is the second functions of clusters which is a fundamental characteristic of them. (Rabenhorst (2009, p. 25 f).

To concretise this description of the different meanings of the terms network and cluster the next chapter is about clusters that exist in business today.

5.2. Strategic Business Clusters

Strategic business clusters are formed with different motivations and in different ways. This chapter shows how clusters work in daily business and why they become a more and more important fact for the choice of location for a company.

5.2.1. Formation and Types of Business Clusters

The motivation for forming a business cluster can be different. There are emergent business cluster like the steel industry in the "Ruhrgebiet" or clusters which organized themselves as a cluster. Business development on economical-political grounds also support the formation of a cluster (Perry 2005, p. 11 ff).
There are vertical and horizontal business clusters. Members of vertical clusters represent the value-added chain of a specific business. An example for such a cluster is given in this assignment in chapter 5.3.2.

Members of vertical business clusters are often dependent on each other.

Horizontal business clusters consist of members in the same level of the value-added chain. Such a cluster is per example a great shopping mall.

5.2.2. More than an Accumulation of Alike Companies

Henry Ford said once (Wirtschaftszitate 2009):

> "Coming together is a start,
> Staying together is an improvement,
> Working together is a success."

Reflecting this quotation from Henry Ford, who lived from 1863 to 1947, you may imagine how important clusters for a successful business are.

Having a first view at a business cluster than you may associate the following with the members of the cluster (Schiele 2003, p. 27):

Members of business cluster are companies that ...

... are more profitable than others in their business
... all belong to the same business
... are all located in the same region

On the one hand this first view approves the definition which is basis of this part of the assignment, the definition of Michael E. Porter. On the other hand there is one new fact that has to be analysed, the association that members of clusters are more profitable or let's say more successful than others. This analysis will be done in chapter 5.2.3. of this assignment.

Before answering the question if a cluster-membership is a strategic advantage and improves therefore the success of the members, let's go back to Porters definition of the term.

Porter (1998, p. 72) shows in his determinants of national advantage, four elements that are needed for a business cluster:

- Firm strategy, structure and rivalry
- Factor conditions
- Demand conditions
- Related and supporting industries

All four elements are interacting in a geographically proximal area.

The figure below visualise this interacting model.

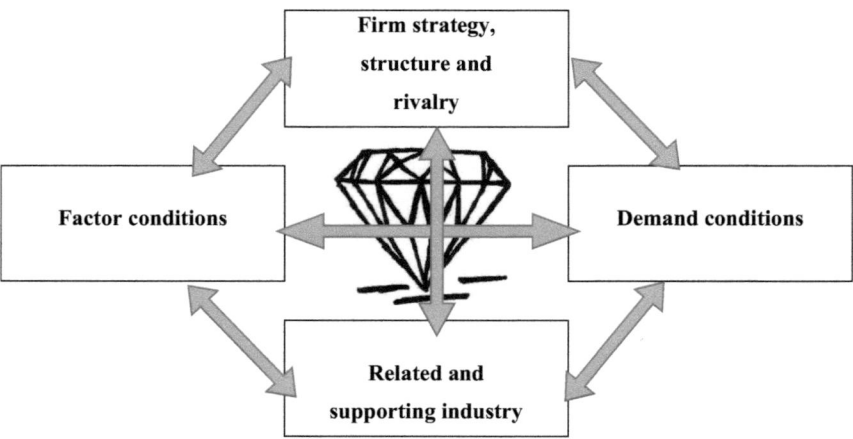

Figure 6: The Determinants of National Advantage (Source: Porter 1998, p. 72)

Factor conditions mean the local availability of labour, capital, natural resources e. g. raw materials as well as the scientific and technological infrastructure (Porter 1998, p. 73 f).

Local customers that are innovative and demanding are covered by the element demand conditions. Demanding and innovative customers are asking for innovative products and services. The settlement of these challenging claims dares the offering members of the cluster being highly innovative and efficient (Porter 1998, p. 99).

Related and supporting industries are strengthening the competiveness of the local companies. The goods and services of diverse suppliers, consultants and engineers are input for the local companies (Porter 1998, p. 100 f).

The fourth element of firm strategy, structure and rivalry fancy the stimulatory competition within the cluster. Companies that are always confronted with their competitor are forced to improve their products and services permanent (Porter 1998, p. 107 f).
All four elements emphasise the first evaluation that members of business clusters are more competitive and therefore more successful than companies that are not in a cluster.

5.2.3. Cluster Membership as Strategic Advantage

The object of investigation in this chapter of the assignment is the success of cluster members. Are business cluster members more successful than companies out of the cluster? Is a business cluster membership a strategic advantage?

Even the interaction between local competitors, their customers and suppliers as well as the supporting infrastructure in the cluster makes the success of such a areal accumulation (Bundesministerium für Bildung und Forschung 2007, p. 2).

Schiele (2003, p. 28 f) wrote that the structure of a cluster itself is a factor for more successful members in the cluster.

A business cluster consists of following members:

- several competitors
- important customers
- their suppliers and
- supporting infrastructure

Often there are the toughest rivals in the cluster. This pushes the competitors to be innovative to be more innovative than the rival and therefore being more successful and competitive than companies outside the cluster. Companies outside the cluster often realise the demand for innovation too late because they do not feel in such an early stage the force to develop their products and services than the cluster members do.

Demanding customers in a business cluster are, let's call them trendsetters. They anticipate international trends. This strengthens the competing companies in the cluster. The customers in the cluster are challenging the companies. The companies have to react on the ambitious demand that creates an innovative spirit in the business cluster.

Competitive suppliers will complete the value-added chain in the business cluster. Successful companies want to work with competitive suppliers therefore the suppliers have to be also innovative.

Supporting infrastructure is offered by the cluster itself to the members. Examples for this are research and development cooperation with universities, marketing platforms, specialists consulting the members and do not forget the importance of knowing each other. A cluster is also a great platform for communication and information exchange.

There is no miracle it is such simple as written in this few paragraphs. Challenging members can be member of this spiral of success.

For supporting all these theoretical items chapter 5.3. displays two successful clusters.

5.2.4. International Business Clusters?

The question is: Is it possible to form an international business cluster? Every time you read and hear about local clusters. Being local, in a geographical proximity in also an important facts for the definition of the term cluster.

Schiele (2003, p. 72) found no really existing international clusters. He pointed out that geographical proximity has also a cultural dimension. Therefore international clusters are not formed.

Browsing the actual literature you will not find an example for an international cluster. You find a lot of information about the actual trend to set up an internationalisation strategy for clusters. Internationalisation means for clusters to cooperate with foreign clusters or foreign networks.

Roman Noetzel (2008) talked about the internationalisation of clusters at the German cluster-conference in October 2008. He pointed out that the globalisation demands that business clusters should support the internationalisation of their members. Target of this is the enhancement of the competitiveness of the members. The Enterprise Europe Network is one European network that supports this idea.

Now let's have a look at existing business clusters. What is their target? How are they performing. Are they acting international?

5.3. Examples for Business Clusters

As the headline of this chapter tells these are only examples of a wide range of clusters. The first example was chosen because of its geographical proximity. The second example was chosen to display a foreign cluster in a well-known industry.

5.3.1. Cluster EnergieForschung.NRW

In North-Rhine Westphalia energy is more converted and used than in any other province of Germany. Using natural resources is a long tradition in NRW and therefore a great energy technological competence grew up. In NRW you find a dense net of research facilities and a lot of companies that offer innovative energy products and services that increase the energy efficiency. (cef.nrw.de 2009a)

The Cluster EnergieForschung.NRW is an accumulation of research and development in North-Rhine Westphalia. The establishment of new and the expansion of existing research facilities strengthen the strengths of their members.

The target of the cluster is to link the actors of the whole value-added chain. They coordinate the collaboration of research and scientific facilities with the economy (cef.nrw.de 2009b).

5.3.2. ACstyria Autocluster GmbH

The ACstyria Autocluster GmbH was the first automotive cluster in Austria. It was founded in 1995 in Graz. The target of the cluster when it was founded was to link economy, industry, research and public facilities and to encourage strength and synergies sustainable. (ACstyria 2009a) The members of the cluster are from different businesses:

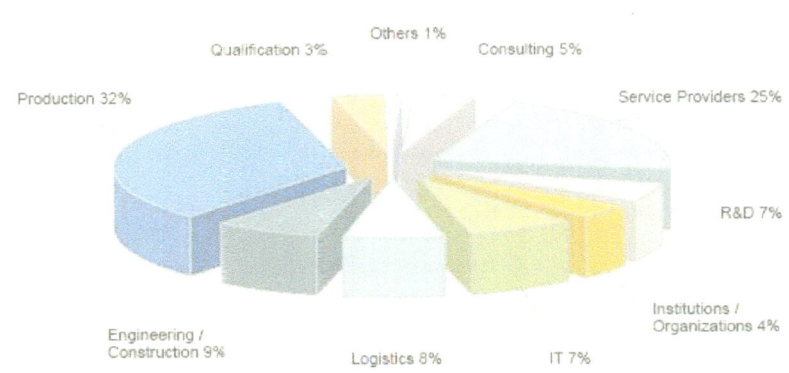

Figure 7: Members of ACstyria (Source: ACstyria.com)

For the future the ACStyria drafted a strategy, called strategy 2011. The strategy 2011 has following slogan: "With automotive power Styria in the future" Going not into detail of the strategy, summarised the ACStyria wants to get their members "fit for the future". This target can be reached by strengthening the competitiveness, the chance on the markets and the power of innovation of the cluster members (ACStyria 2009b).

6 Alliances

6.1. What is an Alliance?

When we refer to alliances in this Chapter, we mean strategic alliances between companies.

A common definition of a strategic alliance is the definition according to Nam-Hoon Kang and Kentaro Sakai (Kang and Sakai 2000, p. 7):

Strategic alliances can have a variety of forms, ranging from an arm's-length contact to a joint venture. But the core of a strategic alliance is an inter-firm co-operative relationship that enhances the effectiveness of the competitive strategies of the participating firms by the trading of mutually beneficial resources such as technologies, skills, etc.

According to Yoshino (1995, in Kang and Sakai 2000, p. 7), strategic alliances have the following three characteristics:

- The two or more firms that unite to pursue a set of agreed goals remain independent subsequent to the formation of the alliance.
- The partner firms share the benefits of the alliance and the control over the performance of assigned tasks.
- The partner firms contribute on basis in one or more key strategic areas, (e. g. technology, products).

Strategic alliances encompass a wide range of inter-firm linkages, including joint ventures, minority equity investments, equity swaps, joint research and development, joint manufacturing, joint marketing, long-term sourcing agreements, shared distribution/services and standards-setting. However, mergers and acquisitions, overseas subsidiaries of multinational corporations, and franchising agreements are not classified as strategic alliances, since they do not involve independent firms with separate goals or call for continuous contribution of participating firms such as transfer of technology or skills between partners.

Alliances are often bound by a single agreement. A very typical example is code sharing in airline alliances.

6.2. Difference between Alliances
6.2.1. Primary Differentiation

The business expert Marc Darby (2006, p. 24) distinguished five basic types of alliances as follows:

- Sales Alliance
- Solution-Specific Alliance
- Geographic-Specific Alliance
- Investment Alliance
- Joint Venture Alliance

This is only a rough overview of the different alliance types. A more comprehensive way to describe business alliances is the "Pyramid of Alliances".

6.2.2. Pyramid of Alliances

The best and most detailed way to describe the structure and difference of alliances is the "Pyramid of Alliances". The pyramid distinguishes different types of alliance structures on the base of three variables: risk, use of staff and costs (Segil 1998, p. 34 ff).

The alliance types at the bottom of the pyramid usually have low risk, a minimal use of staff and low costs. Therefore it is easy to start an alliance at this level, even for small or medium-sized businesses. From bottom up risks, use of staff and costs increases. As a result of that, the higher categories are in general only interesting for bigger, well-off enterprises. Mergers or acquisitions possess the highest risk, use of staff and costs as well.

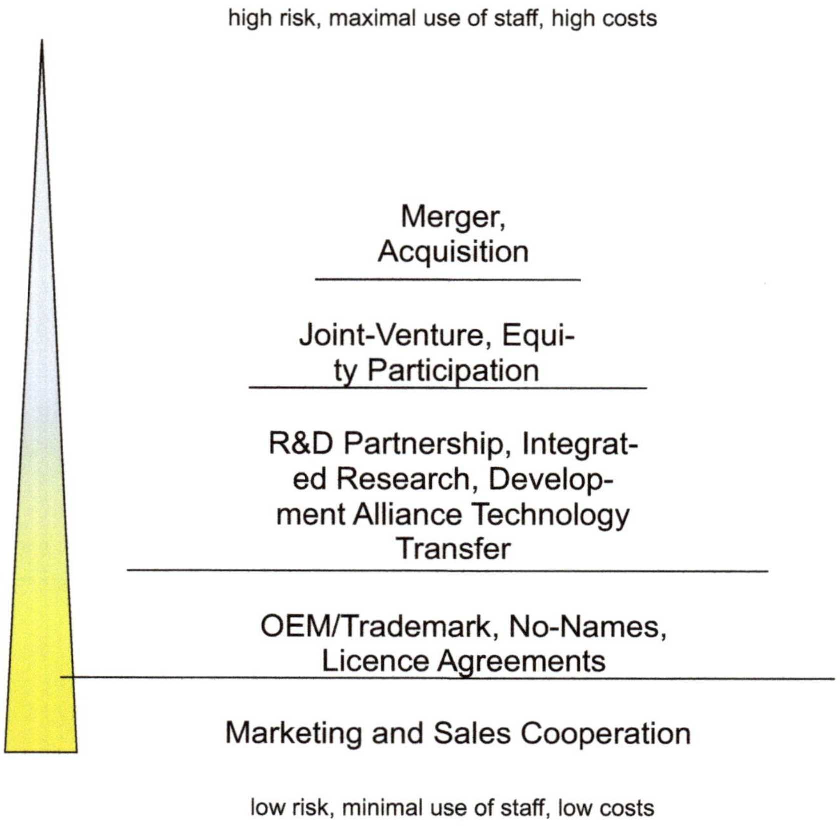

high risk, maximal use of staff, high costs

Merger, Acquisition

Joint-Venture, Equity Participation

R&D Partnership, Integrated Research, Development Alliance Technology Transfer

OEM/Trademark, No-Names, Licence Agreements

Marketing and Sales Cooperation

low risk, minimal use of staff, low costs

Figure 8: Pyramid of Alliances (Source: The Lared Group)

Explanation:

- Merger/Acquisition: a merger describes the fusion of two or more companies, a acquisition the purchase of a whole company or of the capital majority

- Joint-Venture/Equity Participation: in order to start a new, encompassed, division, two companies work together to reach appointed objectives. Equity participation describes the purchase of a part of the equity of another firm. This can be done through cash, exchange of stock or other reward.

- R&D Partnership, Integrated Research, Development Alliance, Technology Transfer: two or more firms work together in a R&D partnership to develop a new technology (i. e. Integrated Research) or/and new products (i. e. Development Alliance) to a mutual advance. Technology transfer happens when one company assigns a second company – for a suitable payment – to use their knowledge and the legal right to use them.

- OEM/Trademark, No-Names, Licence Agreements: OEM means, that one firm produces a product, but others take them to market (especially used in the software industry). Trademarks and No-Names have the same meaning, but these names are predominantly used for consumer goods. With a licence agreement, a company agrees after payment of an initial fee and a certain percentage of the turnover, to use their know-how. The agreement can be limited to a certain technology or geographic region.

- Marketing and Sales Cooperation: two or more companies align with each other to market their products.

6.3. Integration of Alliances in Companies Strategies

More and more companies start up strategic alliances as studies about this subject reveal (Gerybadze 1995, p. 20). These companies are prompted by several motives, including economising on production and research costs, strengthening their market presence and accessing the intangible assets of other firms such as managerial skills and knowledge of markets and customers (Kang and Sakai 2000, p. 31).

Nevertheless, an alliance is not necessarily profitable for all fields of business activities or type of firms.

Besides the financial factor, the alliance has to fit in the company's strategy.

Therefore, the alliance has to be integrated in the company's strategic plan before it starts. The planning of alliances should follow the following steps (Segil 1998, p. 83 ff):

- Development of a strategic plan
- Development of an alliance plan
- Selection of an alliance partner
- Development of an implementation schedule
- Implementation

Without proper planning in advance, a complicated task like a strategic alliance will not be successful.

6.4. Preparation of a Business Alliance

For some companies it is easy to find a suitable alliance partner, for others it is not. If it's not easy to find a partner, the company is well advised to follow Segil's 15-step-plan (1998, p. 142 ff).

1. *Development of qualitative and quantitative criteria to assess possible alliance partner*

   The first step is a proper analysis of the own company's strength with strategic business methods.[1]

2. *Compilation of a list with possible alliance candidates*

   Even if a company is focused on a specific candidate, alternatives should be considered! Sometimes an alliance does not develop according to the planned schedule and as a result of that, an alternative firm is necessary as an alliance partner.

3. *Analysis of strategic concord*

   The alliance itself has not only to fit in your company's strategic plan, it has to fit in the alliance partner's as well. Therefore, this one of the most imported points to check.

4. *Compilation of a ranking list following the result of the strategic concord*

   This should include a list of "spare candidates".

5. *Meeting and assessment of possible alliance candidates*

   A personal contact to the possible partner makes the start of an alliance much easier. Here a management consultant can be helpful as well. The main objective of this initial contact is to get as much information about the company as possible to make the assessment easier.

6. *Supporter of an alliance at the associated company?*

   It is absolutely essential to know a person of the possible partner firm which agrees to the cooperation. By this personal contact, problems are much easier to solve.

7. *Look for hidden risks*

---

[1] These methods are well known and therefore not part of this assignment.

In this step, the legal and financial department or external specialists should scrutinise the whole process.

8. *Intra-company decision*

   A team inside the company must check all pros and cons of the alliance and make a decision about it on the highest management level.

9. *Development of a implementation schedule*

   To realise the project in a considerable time, an implementation schedule has to be developed. All managers responsible for the project are to by named, a timeline has to be fixed.

10. *Try a quick step forward if the associated company tries to delay*

    Sometimes a change of the market draws the whole attention of the alliance partner on it. The aspired cooperation seems to fade away.

    To break the tie, a quick step forward can be the answer. Submit a proposal of an alliance on a low level. This shows the possible partner the high interest in his company and, however, opens possibly the door for further, bigger cooperations.

11. *Apply the "Mindshift-Method[2]" on selected partner*

    This method shows all differences between the senior managers of the two firms. It is essential to have a good agreement between the managers. A 100-percent concord can seldom be acquired, but is it possible to go on even with some disagreements? If these are too big, the alliance is condemned to fail.

12. *Final assessment of all relevant Information before marking of the contract*

    Now all relevant facts are obvious. These should be assessed for last time before the signing the contract. Maybe, meanwhile some facts have changed in the elapsed months. This is the point in the timeline of the alliance were the ranking list of possible partners should be checked for the last time.

13. *Solving all problems before making of the contract*

---

[2] A method developed by the business expert Larraine Segil. This method can be used to diagnose and understand the lifecycle and profile of a company. For more information see: Segil 1998, whole chapter 2, p. 45 ff.

If possible, all problems should be solved before the agreement is signed. Start a meeting with the partner company and talk about problems which could arise in the future.

14. Negotiation of the alliance agreement

At this step the agreement with all details has to be negotiated. Different styles of negotiation are sometimes a problem, in particular in foreign countries. The objective must be to sign a letter of intent (i. e. 'Absichtserklärung').

15. Clarification of a legal questions

Now the contract should be scrutinised by a lawyer familiar with business law. The contract should contain passages about clarifying of conflicts between the two companies

6.5. Examples for Strategic Alliances

6.5.1. Automobile Industry

Not many inventions have changed the world that dramatically like the automobile. Since the first maiden voyage through Bertha Benz in 1888 in an automobile, the automobile sector has changed a lot. There
are not many fields in the world were the
competition is that tough. Therefore, in this business strategic alliances have been the norm for a long time, to be even more competitive.

Car makers mainly use alliances to:

- manufacture certain car parts
- join their R & D activities
- concentrate their sales activities

In the last years there have been about 100 new alliances per year. Most of them are manufacturing joint ventures. Around 80% of them were cross border activities (Kang and Sakai 2000, p. 24).
Some of the alliances are long standing (e. g. Ford/Mazda, General Motors/Isuzu) others are only focused on a particular project (e. g. MAN and VW for manufacturing medium sized trucks).
Several factors are driving (international) alliances in the automobile industry. One is the excess capacity. PricewaterhouseCoopers stated in 1999, that the worldwide car industry has a production capacity of some 20 million vehicles per year (Kang and Sankai 2000, p. 25). Therefore the producers are under high pressure to operate the lines at full capacity.
Nowadays some companies have started R&D projects for environmental-friendly car concepts (e. g. Californian Fuel Cell Partnership (Mercedes, Ford, Honda and Volkswagen)).
Other alliances are generally aiming on partnerships such as the 'Alliance of Automobile Manufacturers Association' which includes eleven major auto manufactures[3].
Despite the recent recession in the industrial nations and therefore falling numbers in car sales, the number in car sales in emerging nations is predicted to grow rapidly.
Due to that fact, the number of alliances in the car industry will rise even more.

---

[3] For more information see: www.autoalliance.org.

6.5.2. Airlines

After World War II, several airlines started its commercial business. In 1952 the British Overseas Aircraft Corporation (BOAC) started its regular service as the first airline with a jet plane. The German Lufthansa followed in 1955, the US-American Pan Am in 1958. Since then, the passenger volume has risen dramatically.

Nowadays the international airline industry is one of the highest regulated in the world. Air routes and their frequency are generally determined by bilateral government agreements. Due to that, airlines must limit the number and range they can service (Kang and Sankai 2000, p. 28).
The airlines focussed mainly on strengthening and expanding their market presence through providing transport possibilities to a lot of destinations around the world.
The consolidation in the airline industry increases. E. g. Air Berlin got in alliance with, or purchased seven airlines in the preceding five years alone (Air Berlin 2009):

- 2004 NIKI
- 2006 dba and Belair
- 2007 LTU and LGW Luftfahrtgesellschaft Walther
- 2008 S7 Airlines and Hainan Airlines

To be competitive in this market, especially due to the high pressure of low-cost-airlines even for old, well known airlines, an airline alliance is often the only way to avoid bankruptcy.

At the moment there are three major airline alliances existing worldwide:

- Star Alliance (24 partner) (Star Alliance 2009)
- Sky Team (13 partner) (Sky Team 2009)
- oneworld Alliance (10 partner) (oneworld 2009)

The market share of the major flight alliances was 57% in 1999 (Economist 1999 in Kang and Sankai 2000) within four bigger alliances. The number now has risen up to 60% in 2009 (oneworld 2009) with only three main alliances remaining.

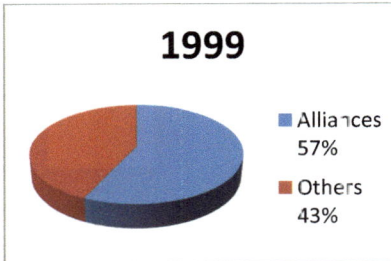 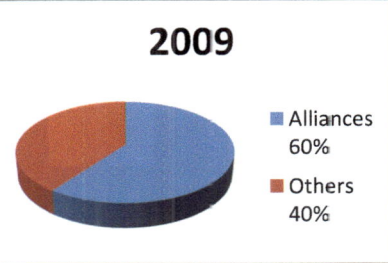

Figure 9: Airline Alliances in 1999 and 2009 (Source: Own Interpretation)

Due to the pressure of further cost saving and the demand of customers for more and more destinations and service, it can be assumed that the number of airlines in alliances will rise even more.

6.6. Future of Alliances

As stated in this subchapter, there is a wide variety of different types of alliances. Some are short lasting, others are long lasting. Some are deeply interwoven others only loosely. However, as Professor Gerybadze[4] (Gerybadze 1995, p. 267 ff) mentioned in his book, five extraordinary driving forces for alliances in the future:

- ecological problems such as the increasing production of CO_2, the deforestation of tropical zones and the related greenhouse-effect can only be solved through decisive and coordinated activities at a global level;

- global competition and the international division of labour will undergo a major restructuring process and will increasingly call for international cooperation and new forms of economic coordination;

- the development and dissemination of fusion technologies increasingly involves companies from different industries, government agencies, research laboratories as well as universities;

---

[4] Professor Dr. Alexander Gerybadze, Professor of Business Administration and Technology Management at St. Gallen University, Switzerland.

- the political and economic transition process in Eastern Europe can only be envisaged as a well-coordinated economic development programme involving governments and private investors in both the Eastern and the Western parts of the world;

- if the North-South conflict is to be resolved, new cooperative solutions are inevitable. The reconsideration of new concepts and the creation of new institutions for economic policy and development aid are of particular concern.

As shown above, in the future there are some difficult global problems to tackle. These challenges can only be solved by cross-border acting strategic company alliances or/and strategic alliances with or between governments.

But not only the 'big problems' are a challenge for firms, the competition in nearly all business sectors is getting tougher every year. To be even more competitive as the competitors, further cost reduction and new business solutions are in demand.

Therefore, the number of alliances will definitely grow further in the subsequent years.

7 Results

There are three good ways for a single company to cope with the new economical circumstance and to remain competitive and perhaps to become a big local and also global player or a part of one:

- the organisation networks
- the business clusters
- the alliances

All three ways imply big opportunities on national and international markets.
Alliances and organisation networks offer the possibility for single companies to act more global than it may be possible for them on their own. Business clusters are mainly locally concentrated but they are often present at international topic relevant fairs or symposium. That is the way business clusters offer international contacts to their members.

8 Conclusion

In future the progress will continue, the innovations of products will increase, the product life-cycles will decrease. Because of this fact it is obvious that an increasing development of organisation networks, business clusters and alliances will take place as well. Only by these means single companies especially on high production levels will have the chance to expand and to survive.

It should be considered to become a member of an organisation network, a business cluster or an alliance already when thinking about and writing down the corporate strategy. Positive effects of such combinations maybe in some cases realized from the beginning of the membership but they are most the time strategic ones.

9 Bibliography

1000Ventures (2009). *Strategic Alliances – Why and How To Build Them.* Available from: http://www.1000ventures.com/business_guide/strategic_alliances _main.html [Accessed 19 September 2009]

ACStyria (2009a). *Wir über uns. Daten & Fakten.* Available from: http://www.acstyria.com/index.php/de_DE/wir-uber-uns/daten-fakten [Accessed 4 October 2009]

ACStyria (2009b). *Der ACStyria.* Available from: http://www.acstyria.com/index.php/de_DE/wir-uber-uns [Accessed 4 October 2009]

Air Berlin (2009). *Über uns.* Available from: http://www.airberlin.com/site/aboutstart.php?LANG=deu [Accessed 24 September 2009]

Alter, C., Hage, J. [1993]. *Organizations working together.* 1. Edition. London: SAGE Publications Inc.

Bartlett, C.A., Ghoshal, S. [1990]. *Internationale Unternehmensführung. Innovation, globale Effizienz, differenziertes Marketing. 1. Auflage.* Frankfurt/Main: Campus.

Bundesministerium für Bildung und Forschung (2007). *Deutschlands Spitzencluster. Mehr Innovation. Mehr Wachstum. Mehr Beschäftigung.* Bonn: BMBF

Darby, Mark (2006). *Alliance Brand – Fulfilling the Promise of Partnering.* West Sussex: John Wiley & Sons Ltd.

De Rond, Mark (2003). *Strategic Alliances as Social Facts.* Cambridge: Cambridge University Press

Cluster EnergieForschung.NRW (2009a). *Energieforschung in NRW.* Available from: http://www.cef.nrw.de/page.asp?TopCatID=11747&RubrikID=11747 [Accessed 4 October 2009]

Cluster EnergieForschung.NRW (2009b). *Das Cluster*. Available from: http://www.cef.nrw.de/page.asp?TopCatID=11746&RubrikID=11746 [Accessed 4 October 2009]

Duden (2006). *Fremdwörterbuch, Band 5*. 9th edition. Mannheim: Bibliographisches Institut & E.A. Brockhaus AG

Eschenbach, Rolf, Eschenbach, Sebastian and Kunesch Hermann (2003). *Strategische Konzepte. Management-Ansätze von Ansoff bis Ulrich*. 4th edition. Stuttgart: Schäffer-Poeschel Verlag

Gerybadze, Alexander (1995). *Strategic Alliances and Process Redesign – Effective Management and Restructuring of Cooperative Projects and Networks*. Berlin: Walter de Gruyter & Co.

Grote Westrick, Dagmar and Rehfeld Dieter (2003). *Cluster (Standortverbünde) in der Region Rheinland*. Gelsenkirchen: Institut Arbeit und Technik

Heilemann Ullrich and Weihs Claus (2007). *Classification and Clustering in business Cycle Analysis*. Heft 79 Berlin: Duncker & Humbolt GmbH

Heller, Robert (2006). *Business Alliances: Working with your business competitors instead of against them*. Available from: http://www.thinkingmanagers.com/management/business-alliances.php [Accessed 19 September 2009]

Kang, Nam-Honn and Sakai, Kentaro (2000). *International Strategic Alliances – Their Role in Industrial Globalisation*. Paris: OECD

Kutschker, Michael, Schmid, Stefan [1995]. *Netzwerke internationaler Unternehmungen. Diskussionsbeitrag Nr. 64 der Wirtschaftswissenschaftlichen Fakultät*. Ingolstadt: Kath. Universität Eichstätt.

Langenscheidt (2009). *Cluster*. Available from: http://services.langenscheidt.de/fremdwb/fremdwb.html [Accessed 2 October 2009]

Lee, Hyun Young (2005). *Strategic Alliances and Trade Dispute in Automobile Industry*. Toyama: Centre for Far Eastern Studies, Toyama University

Maier, Gunther and Tödtling, Franz (2006). *Regional- und Stadtökonomik 1*. 4th edition. Wien: Springer-Verlag

Marshall, Alfred (1905). *Handbuch der Volkswirtschaftslehre*

Noetzel, Roman (2008). *Internationalisierungsstrategien für Cluster*. Available from: http://www.clusterkonferenz.de/uploads/media/Praes_Noetzel_Forum_A.pdf [Accessed 4 October 2009]

Oneworld (2009). *An introduction to oneworld: The alliance that revolves around you*. Available from: http://www.oneworld.comcontentfactsheetW2_2009-02-03%20introduction%20to%20oneworld.pdf [Accessed 22. September 2009]

Park, Soon-Chan (2000). *Makroökonomisches Wachstum und geographische Agglomeration*. Frankfurt am Main: Peter Lang GmbH Europäischer Verlag der Wissenschaft

Perry, Martin (2005). *Business Clusters. An international perspective*. New York: Routledge

Plattner, Michael (2001). *Cluster-Evolution im Produktionssystem der ostdeutschen Halbleiterindustrie*. Band 21. Münster: LIT Verlag

Porter, Michael, E. (1998). *The Competitive Advantage of Nations*. Hampshire and London: Macmillan Press Ltd.

Porter, Michael, E. (1999). *Wettbewerbsstrategie*. 10th edition. Frankfurt am Main: Campus Verlag GmbH

Powell, W.W. [1987]. *Hybrid organizational arrangements: New form or transactional development?*. In: California Management Review [1/1987, pp. 67-87]. Vol. 30. Berkeley: University of California.

Rabenhorst, Hans-Christian (2009). *Service-Erwartungen und Leistungsbündel in Chemie-Clustern*. Düsseldorf: Düsseldorfer University Press

Sain, S. [2009]. *Lecture notes of International Management (International Strategy)*, Winter Session 2009-2010. 1st edition. Düsseldorf: FOM, MBA.

Schiele, Holger (2003). *Der Standort-Faktor.* Weinheim: Wiley-VCH GmbH & Co. KGaA

Segil, Larraine (1998). *Strategische Allianzen – Systematische Planung und Durchführung von Unternehmensallianzen* Zürich: Midas Management Verlag AG

Sellien, R., Sellien, H. (1988). Gabler Wirtschafts-Lexikon, Taschenbuch-Kasette mit 6 Bänden, 12. Auflage, Wiesbaden: Gabler.

Sky Team (2009). *SkyTeam Livery Fact Sheet.* Available from: http://www.skyteam.com/downloads/news/facts/skyteamFactSheet.pdf [Accessed 24. September 2009]

Small Business Notes (2009). *Strategic Alliances.* Available from: http://www.smallbusinessnotes.com/operating/leadership/strategicalliances.html [Accessed 19. September 2009]

Star Alliance (2009). *Mitgliedsgesellschaften.* Available from: http://www.staralliance.com/de/about/airlines/ [Accessed 24. September 2009]

Sydow, J. (1991). *Unternehmensnetzwerke: Begriffe, Erscheinungsformen und Implikationen für die Mitbestimmung,* Manuskript Nr. 30 der Hans-Böckler-Stiftung, Düsseldorf: Hans-Böckler-Stiftung.

Sydow, J. (1992a). *Strategische Netzwerke: Evolution und Organisation.* 1. Auflage. Wiesbaden: Gabler.

Sydow, J. (1992b). *Strategische Netzwerke und Transaktionskosten,* in: Staehle, W.H., Conrad, P.: Managementforschung. Berlin: De Gruyter.

Sydow, J. (1995a). *Netzwerkorganisation. Interne und externe Restrukturierung von Unternehmen, in: Wirtschaftswissenschaftliches Studium,* Heft 12. München: Verlag C.H. Beck OHG.

Sydow, J. (1995). *Netzwerkbildung und Kooperation als Führungsaufgabe*. In: Kieser, A., Reber, G., Wunderer, R. [1995]. Handwörterbuch der Führung. 2. Auflage. Stuttgart: Schäffer-Poeschel Verlag.

Thompson, A.A, Strickland, A.J. Gamble, J.E. (2008). Crafting & Executing Strategy – The *Quest for Competitive Advantage*. 16th Edition. New York: McGraw-Hill.

Thorelli, H.B. (1986). *Networks: Between Markets and Hierarchies*. In: Strategic Management Journal, Vol. 7. United Kingdom: Strategic Management Society.

Verst, D. (2009). *Geschäftsmodell für Soziale Netze ist endlich gefunden*. Available from: http://www.seedfinance.de/2009/01/05/geschaeftsmodell-fuer-soziale-netze-ist-endlich-gefunden/ [Accessed 3 November 2009].

Wildemann, H. (1998). Entwicklungs-, Produktions- und Vertriebsnetzwerke, Delphi-Studie. 1. Auflage. München: TCW Transfer-Centrum GmbH & Co. KG.

Wirtschaftszitate (2009). *Henry Ford*. Available from http://www.wirtschaftszitate.de/autor/ford_henry.php [Accessed 03 October 2009]

World technology evaluation center WTEC (2009). *Loyola – International Technology Research Institute*. Available from: http://www.wtec.org/loyola/polymers/fh7_16.gif [Accessed 30.10.2009].

Zdrowomyslaw, Norbert and Bladt, Michael (2009). *Regionalwirtschaft. Global denken, lokal und regional handeln*. Gernsbach: Deutscher Betriebswirte-Verlag GmbH